Mish Mash

Written & illustrated by

R Kaur

Published by R Kaur

© Copyright 2024 R Kaur

www.instagram.com/rkaur.expression
rkaur.expression@gmail.com

The rights of R Kaur to be identified as the author of this work have been asserted by her in accordance with the Copyright, Designs and Patents Act of 1988.

All rights reserved; no part of this publication may be reproduced, stored in a retrieval system, or transmitted in any form or by any means, electronic, mechanical, photocopying, recording or otherwise without the prior written consent of the publisher or a licence permitting copying in the UK issued by the Copyright Licensing Agency Ltd, www.cla.co.uk

ISBN 978-1-78792-055-2

Book design, layout and production management by Into Print
www.intoprint.net
+44 (0)1604 832149

"NO COLOUR HAS A SINGLE SHADE".

Through my writing, I hope to convey the message that we all must embrace what makes us unique. To learn to accept and nurture what makes us different.
Only then can new shades begin to flourish.
The beauty of our oddities adds richness to the stew x

Acknowledgements

A special thank you, as always, to my daughter Saraa.

To Dad for your philosophical offerings and to mum, for your mish mash of richness, strength, and perseverance. Thank you to Mum and Papa Ji x.

Thank you to Klash Singh (Mum Ji), a feminist like no other, and to family, for being mine x.

Thank you to Jack Ward for your advice on Mish Mash from a religious and cultural perspective. This was a key area of focus for me, and your comments are greatly valued.

Thank you to Anita Radden, Emma Beasley and Rahena Khanum for your contribution to the perspectives and connections to the topics covered. Thank you to Bobby Puncher and Laura O'Neil for your grammatical expertise and comments on the topics covered in Mish Mash.

A special thank you to all those who have offered their advice and sentiments on the topics included in the book over the years. To all those who have added positivity, richness, and insight to my journey in the writing of this book.

A special thank you to Jasdev for the advice you have offered through your words, actions, and experiences. Priceless xx

Contents

Author's message..............................3

Introduction: Let's Go! 7

Chapter 1. Identity

Religion, tradition, or culture? 13
Trio of traditions 15
Roman Road Market......................16
Edinburgh 17

Chapter 2. Change

From woman, man is born................21
Diasporic beauty 22
Arranged marriages......................25
Framed 27
Tharan..................................28
Change..................................30
My other half............................31
Power...................................32
Freedom 33
Pages 34
Rekindling of an old flame................35

About the author.......................... 39

Introduction

Let's go!

So, when life creeps up on you, life creeps up on you. BOOM!

This has been a long-awaited moment for me. Drum roll please...

Now, before I continue, it's important to clarify a few things. I want my readers to delve into these mind-boggling, head-spinning, comical twists and turns, and at times, more touching, deeper tones with a clear understanding of what it is that I've set out to achieve.

The following pages are a mish mash of thoughts, feelings, events, experiences, and memories which I have accumulated over the many moons of my existence. Some of which are my own and some of which belong to others. Which ones belong to whom... now that would be telling!

They are, if you will, a collection of utter randomness put together in the form of yet more utter randomness. This is because, to me, life does not follow a simple narrative. It's one event after another that simply does not blend in neatly with the other.

To me, that's the beauty of it. I am an abstract thinker. I have come to the understanding that I enjoy life best when the dots don't join. When the ruler that we so well intentionally position to guide us on our path suddenly slips and creates a new and rather disjointed path for us to continue on our way.

The following pages are a collection of topics aimed at provoking deeper thought and discussion. Female identity being at the heart. Mish Mash focuses on cultural and societal influences on female identity. These topics have been presented through a mish mash of mediums, from prose, poetry to pictures.

Take today, for instance. I woke up at 05:30 with the intention of going for a training run, only to decide that I was too achy from yesterday's run. So, I decided a quick weight training session would compensate. I then looked over to my desk and felt a guilty, sinking sensation in my stomach because I'd been planning to work on my university assignment at least one day before work that week, and Friday was fast approaching.

What I decided to do instead, was have a ridiculously quick stretching session (if you can even call it a session-it was so quick!). I suddenly felt a huge sense of relief at having talked myself out of a training run and a weight training session because I now had something very important to work on.

I poured myself some cereal (because I couldn't even be bothered to make myself my usual breakfast of porridge) and made myself my morning brew to set me up for the day (Yorkshire tea, of course, a proper brew!).

I settled down at my desk and opened my textbook. Without even realising it, a few precious sips of my tea; and my soothing morning beverage had taken me into a trance-like state of wonder and imagination. I found myself from one moment reading Plato's Laches to tapping random waffle on my laptop, to…

Well, here we are!

As you can see, setting out a plan doesn't always mean we're going to stick to it.

Going back to the notion that 'my glass is always half full' reminded me that although I hadn't completed my to-do list for that morning, I had at least made a good start on writing this book, which had left me with a feeling of great satisfaction and excitement, that it had finally started coming together! (At least, I thought it had – perhaps you might be thinking that I really should have gone for that training run or continued reading Plato's Laches after all!) Nevertheless, the moral of the story is that life takes unexpected twists and turns, which can lead to unexpectedly positive outcomes. (Sounds like Plato's rubbing off on me!).

But enough of the philosophical talk; there's plenty of time for that. Let us begin by delving deep into my concoction of thought-provoking anecdotes and poems.

Now, turn the pages and delve deeper with me…

Chapter 1. Identity

Religion, tradition, or culture?

Religion, tradition, or culture. The fine line between these three mesmerizing concepts was so often an entanglement in my mind. I've always loved the idea of religion, tradition, and culture, but honestly, when I was younger, I couldn't distinguish between them. But in the rare moments that I could, I felt as if tradition and culture were hindering my understanding of religion.

However, in more recent times, I'm pleased to say I have come to an understanding that it is not so much an 'entanglement' but more of a delicate intertwining of ideas, beliefs, and practices that have been formulated as a result of the merger between the three.

I have come to the humble understanding that religion is a set of beliefs that, dependent upon which part of this beautiful planet you have been brought up in, will have a different set of traditions and cultural practices. Therefore, inevitably, interpretations will differ in the practice of beliefs being observed and taught because of differences in lifestyles.

The moral of the story that I have come up with on my voyage of discovery thus far in life is that I love religion, culture, and tradition, and the interwoven nature of all three only serves to make them richer.

In my mind, that all makes a lot of sense! (Apologies if I have boggled your minds; I promise the next chapter will be lighter reading!)

Trio of traditions

A Punjabi, born and raised in East London with part Scottish heritage. If that's not a nod to the very sentiment of Mish Mash, I don't know what is.

Fusion is my friend.

The mixture and merger of cultures and traditions is fascinating. A spicy roast dinner on a Sunday evening, laid out on a tartan tablecloth, polished off with an evening's viewing of EastEnders.

Yes, I know what you're thinking, "Wow, she really did grow up in the height of fusion fantasy!" Well, someone had to!

I guess I was just lucky that way.

But on a serious note, the concoction is priceless.

Roman Road Market

Roman Road market on a Saturday morning for a weekend bargain shop. Fruit and veg from a market stall really is something supermarket shopping can never compete with. Chris, my neighbour and market stall holder, would shout his weekly slogan across the length of the market, "Apples and pears, five for a pand, better than any supermarket brand!"

Priceless.

A browse at the stall that sold those dodgy designer bags (that would always fall apart!) was a must. Collecting your bargain buys and ending the trip with the most amazing fish and chips from the chippie at the top of the market. Golden memories.

"Thank you, East London, ya the best."

Edinburgh

Mish Mash is a shout-out to the things close to my heart. I would feel as though I have done myself a disservice if I left out a chapter on my mother's homeland and a real chunk of my heart, Scotland. Specifically, the beauty that is Edinburgh. This is a must. Where to begin?

If you are ever heading up towards the North of Great Britain, I highly recommend you take a pit stop and make her acquaintance.

Amidst the many beauties that this 'bonnie lass' has to offer, some of the fondest are the summer treks up to the spectacular peak of the rough and rugged beauty of Arthur's seat. An extinct volcano that paints a majestic backdrop against the bustling cityscape of Edinburgh. As you descend, you'll discover the prestigious shopping centre along the famous Princess Street.

Walking along Edinburgh's famous cobbled pavements and her beautiful grey stoned architecture, you'll enjoy the sound of bagpipes and the shops selling every colour combination of tartan imaginable...

Other memories include sliding down Calton Hill on sheets of cardboard at dangerously high speed, just for a laugh. Summer holiday traditions...

One of the fondest and most nostalgic memories, however, has got to be of Antigua Street. It is home to the greatest chippie in the world. Scottish tatties rock! The blend of those chips with that Scottish brown sauce (yes, brown sauce) with a side of haggis was harmonious. (I say was, because now I know exactly what haggis is! Sorry, mum!).

When it comes to Scottish tatties vs Eastend chippies, it's a close call, but Eastend chippies will be pipped to the post every time. (Sorry Dad, 1-0 to Mum!). If you ever get the chance, stop by the chippie on Antigua Street, you won't regret it.

Chapter 2. Change

From woman, man is born

*Bhand Jammee-Ai Bhand Nimmee-
Ai Bhand Mangan Vee-Aahu.
Bhandahu Hovai Dostee Bhandahu
Chalai Raahu.
Bhand Mu-Aa Bhand Bhaalee-Ai Bhand Hovai Bandhaan.
So Ki-O Mandaa Aakhee-Ai Jit Jameh
Raajaan.
Bhandahu Hee Bhand Oopjai Bhandai
Baajh Na Ko-Ay.*

*"From woman, man is born,
With woman, man is
Conceived, to woman he is engaged and married.
Woman becomes his friend,
Through woman, the future generations come.
When his woman dies, he seeks
another woman; to who he is
bound.
So why call her bad? From her,
Kings are born.
From woman, woman is born,
without woman, there would be
no one at all."
(Ang 473)
Guru Granth Sahib Ji*

Diasporic Beauty

The beauty in my face
*   is not in the curl of my lash*
*   as I bat my eye.*
*   The beauty in my face*
is not in the arch of my brow
*   or in the curve of my neck,*
*   nor in the features that distinguish me.*
*   It is the look I carry,*
*   the look I bare.*
*   The look of a woman*
*   descended from women,*
*   women dispersed over sporadic lands,*
*   without choice they settled elsewhere.*

*   Grandmothers,*

*   it is your beauty I carry*
*   your beauty I bare.*
I am radiant with your resilience and resolve.

*   I am strong in this land*
you came to share.
*   It is your victory over struggles,*
*   that has blessed me with the beauty I bare.*

*   I am a diasporic woman,*
*   that is me,*
* I am she.*

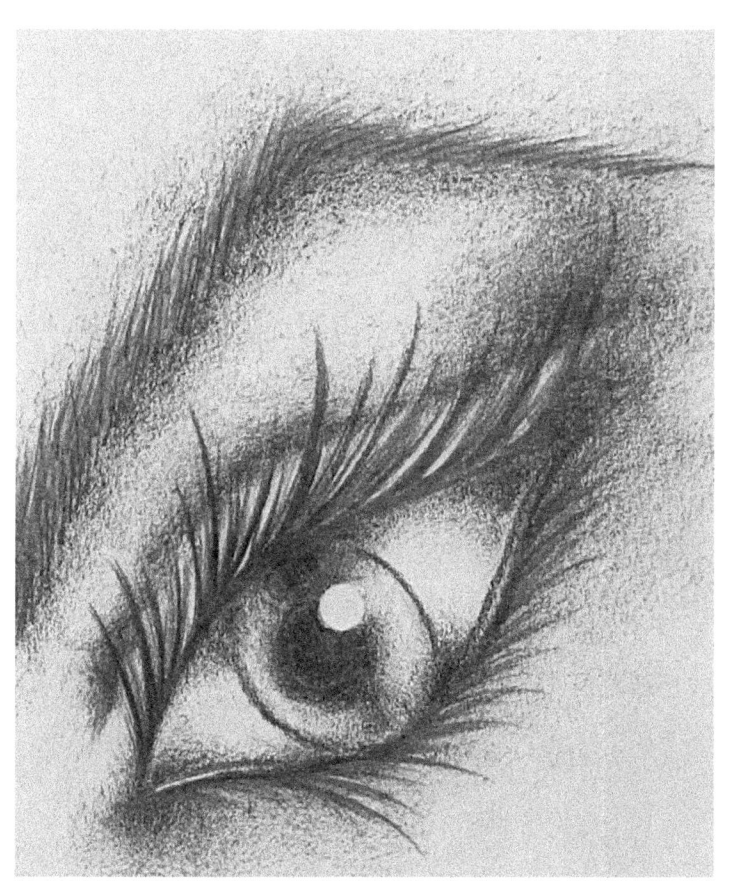

'Arranged' Marriages

Arranged marriages. Where do I begin...

This chapter of Mish Mash was left unwritten for quite some time. In truth, it was a chapter I strongly considered erasing altogether. That, however, would have gone against the purpose of Mish Mash. The purpose being, to paint the fullest picture of life's experiences by selecting topics close to my heart, whether they are my own experiences or those of others which have struck an emotive chord within me.

Whether they fill the heart with joy, or at times, they simply fill it with a random mixture of emotions...

It's taken time and a great deal of reflection to come to the conclusion that the concept of 'arranged' marriages is one which must, like all areas of life, be adapted in order to harmonise with the present.

The term 'arranged' has been highlighted here as, in many cultures, there are differing interpretations. My reference to the word 'arranged' refers to those involved, being judged and even outcast if they were to question or to opt out of the 'arrangement...' due to societal/cultural expectations.

Arranged marriages stemmed from traditional and cultural ways of life, which, for the most part, probably worked for that period (many years ago). Although, in my experience, they have struggled at times to adapt and change over generations.

I am in no way opposed to arranged marriages, but it is necessary to highlight areas that I feel need a light to be shone upon them. Many arranged marriages work and blessed be those that do. For those, however, who have struggled or experienced the emotional friction that can be attached to them, I am speaking to voice those experiences. To echo those voices which struggle to speak due to the consequences and controversies that may follow.

It is also to highlight the importance of change and adaptation. To leave behind tradition and culture is, in my mind, a great loss. It strips the world of its identity. Leaving behind a bland canvas. A universal emptiness. Culture and tradition add colour and emotion; these are fundamental elements of society. But it is crucial that it adapts... It is a celebration of growth and is the root of a 'healthier' society-particularly for specific members of society. Women, at the forefront.

Topics of passion are intense, so much so that it is often easier to overlook them altogether.

Persistence of passion prevails. Change is inevitable.

Framed

Put you in a frame
and tell you your aim.
You're the face of beauty, honesty, and utmost modesty.
You embody these charms,
continue on your way
      and do no harm.

          But...

                my frame was bent
                out of line.

I asked for help

      no one was sent.

            for all that you've installed in me
why can't you seem to see
      there's more than just a frame to me?

Tharan

Glossary: **Tharan** *– Punjabi name meaning saviour*

It is through my story I tell a thousand tales. Think of me as a vessel for voices unsung. The countless wants, needs, and dreams untouched and unspoken. Experiences that were never meant to be shared for the shame they may bear. Do not be mistaken; this is not a story that carries a heavy weight or a sombre tone.

Instead, it shines a light on the things in life that are less expressed. Tones untouched, voices that carry difference in their words. Words less familiar to our comforting vocabulary. Words that bring change. Words to amend, refashion, and refine. Questioning perhaps society's long standing stereotypical design.

Take a deep breath. I am Tharan. This is my voice, and I don't hold back...

Tharan is my voice. I am the voice. Not just for you, or me, but for every woman. I was born and raised just like you. I feel fear, shame, hate, and love.

Young or old; married or single. It makes no difference to me. I'll tell it as I see it, better yet as I feel it. We are all women. One and all. Whether you see it or not. Whether through ignorance or by choice, you are me, and I am you. So, let's begin this journey, written by both you and I.

In life, you play the cards you're dealt. In my humble opinion, I played a good hand despite having been dealt a few jokers of the pack. I wore my poker face until my cards had played their last round...

    I rolled with the punches...

I'm a woman; that's just what we do...

    Why is it women seem to reap far less than they sow?

Chapters build stories. Each year is a chapter, and every day is a page. Read my pages, line by line, beginning to end. Read the magic of my pages.

Pages that built my days.

    Learn my story from beginning to end.

        May I pass on the magic of my pages,

    and may our story have no end...

Change

Change is difference
> *to adjust*
>> *to explore.*

Change is a road that takes us afar.
> *Change is a journey unknown.*
>> *Change is the door left ajar.*
> *Change is the canvas*
>> *waiting to be adorned.*

Change is to amend,
> *refashion,*
>> *reshape*
>>> *and refine.*
> *Change is reform.*

Change is good,
> *it's just misunderstood.*

My other half

You needn't be by my side
    if you feel the need to be the other half of me.
        That half is really quite complete.
I've filled it over the years
    with ambition, strength, love, and laughter.

If you feel the need to be part of me,
    it's simply to keep me company.

Power

Power is strength
Power is dominance.
Power is chiselled and defined.
Power is big, broad, and bold.

Or so I've been told...

My power,
is in my core.
In my stance and my grounding.

My power
is defiance observed through humility.

Power is rooted in principles of humility, virtue, and grace,
no heavy hand could ever take its place.

Freedom

The greatest gift we can bestow upon our daughters
    is freedom,
and of the many freedoms,
        mine chose
           'choice'

    "A wise decision."

Pages

To write is to flood the page with an entanglement of thought.
Words fill pages
  which build paragraphs.
    From here we create chapters
      and eloquently chisel the construction of novels.
        Leaving behind turrets of knowledge
          which stand tall throughout the ages.

As sacred texts are immersed with poetic verses,
  the writers rained their words and drenched and blessed the pages.
        Standing strong
            throughout the ages.
Words that teach of wisdom, virtue, and grace
    blessed be the pages,
      set in stone, which can never be replaced.

Pages

Rekindling of an old flame

In lockdown I stumbled upon you
*   a love I'd once lost.*

Caught
*   in the monotony of isolation.*
*   Sat at my desk*
*   I penned my paper,*
*   and inked my thoughts.*
*   and there you were.*

*   Words...*

*   They mingle, they mutter*
at times they tend to stutter.
*   Intertwined*
*   brushing paths.*

*   In twos or threes,*
*   each sings a different tune.*
Some short
*   some long*
*   enriched with utter depth and flavour.*
Full bodied.
*   Gentle,*
at times they tangle and muddle.

Stuck in a rut,
 but no worry
 erase and start again.
  No rush
   no hurry,
enjoy their breath
 their dance.
  As they swing
 as they sway
  on the pages they glide.

Their angelic bodies
 pitter
 patter

evoke emotion at its height.
 The melody of thought
 the harmony of feelings,
  blessed be the pages they lie upon.

   Words...
    my love x

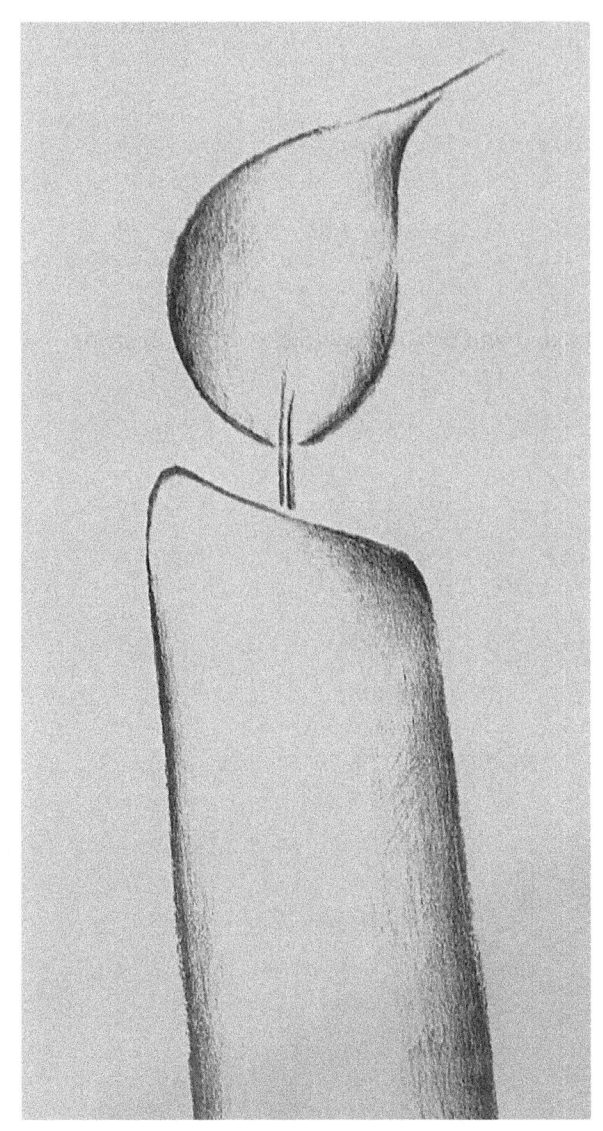

And so, I end this tale with the fullest of stops.

About the author

Rajwant Kaur is a British Indian. Born and raised in Tower Hamlets, East London.

A Teacher of Religious studies. A lover of fitness, travel and creativity.

Her writing spans across genres. Her latest title, *Mish Mash* focuses on cultural and societal influences on the topic of female identity.

www.ingramcontent.com/pod-product-compliance
Lightning Source LLC
Chambersburg PA
CBHW061348040426
42444CB00011B/3139